Little Mitchie

IT TASTES SWEET

LET'S LEARN ABOUT FLAVORS

Kim Thompson

CREATING YOUNG NONFICTION READERS

Little Mitchie books spark curiosity and support early nonfiction reading for students in Grades 2-3. Designed to build vocabulary, support second language learners, and prepare readers for middle-grade content, each book includes helpful tips for parents and educators to build confidence and deepen understanding of the world.

TIPS FOR READING NONFICTION WITH BEGINNING READERS

Talk about Nonfiction

Begin by explaining that nonfiction books give us information that is true. The book will be organized around a specific topic or idea, and we may learn new facts through reading.

Look at the Parts

Most nonfiction books have helpful features. Our *Little Mitchie* titles include color photographs and graphic aids, a table of contents, a glossary, and an index. Share the purpose of these features with your reader.

Color Photos and Graphic Aids

A lot of information can be found by "reading" photos, charts, maps, and other graphic aids found within nonfiction texts. Help your reader learn more about the different ways information can be displayed.

Table of Contents

Located at the front of the book, this list shows the big ideas within the text and the page numbers where they can be found.

Glossary

Located at the back of the book, the glossary defines key words and phrases that are related to the topic. These words and phrases can be found in the text in colored type.

Index

Located at the back of the book, an index is an alphabetical list of topics and the page numbers where they can be found.

With a little help and guidance about reading nonfiction, you can feel good about introducing a young reader to the world of *Little Mitchie* nonfiction books.

Little Mitchie is an imprint of:

Mitchell Lane
PUBLISHERS

2001 SW 31st Avenue
Hallandale, FL 33009
mitchelllanepub.com

First Edition, 2027.

Author: Kim Thompson
Designer: Bobbie Houser

Library of Congress Cataloging-in-Publication Data
Title: It Tastes Sweet / by Kim Thompson

Description: Hallandale, FL :
Mitchell Lane Publishers, [2027]

Identifiers:
ISBN 979-8-89260-858-9 (library bound)
ISBN 979-8-89260-955-5 (eBook)

Library of Congress Control Number: 2026935872

PHOTO CREDITS
Shutterstock: Moni 8005, cover, 1, 3, 4, 10, 18; evgeeenius, 5; ZeiMomArt, 7; Photoongraphy, 8; artem evdokimov, 11; Alexandre Rizzon, 12; Rawpixel.com, 15; Fractal Pictures, 17; New Africa, 19; anna.argentuma, 20; Inside Creative House, 21; Jeannine Schmitte, 22.

TABLE OF CONTENTS

Chapter One

SWEET!

Imagine a shop filled with sweets. There are lollipops, caramels, taffy, and other candies. There may be treats like cupcakes and cookies.

The foods have different shapes, colors, and textures. They have one flavor in common, though. They are all sweet!

TASTY TIDBIT

"We eat first with our eyes" is an old saying. It means that people like food that looks good. Fresh food often has bright colors.

Foods with a sweet flavor are all around us. Some are found in nature. Honey is sweet. Maple syrup comes from sweet tree sap. Fruits and berries burst with sweetness.

Many plants are naturally sweet. They include sugarcane, corn, peas, and beets.

Some sweet foods are made by people. Sugarcane and other plants are **refined** to make the white sugar crystals you buy at the store. This sugar is added to foods to make them sweet.

TASTY TIDBIT

Refined sugar is found in many **processed** foods.

Chapter Two

THE SCIENCE OF SWEETNESS

Sweet foods contain different sugar **molecules**. Fructose is in fruit. Glucose is found in foods like rice and potatoes. Sucrose is table sugar. It has both fructose and glucose.

TASTY TIDBIT

You need sugar to survive. It is the body's main source of energy. It fuels the brain.

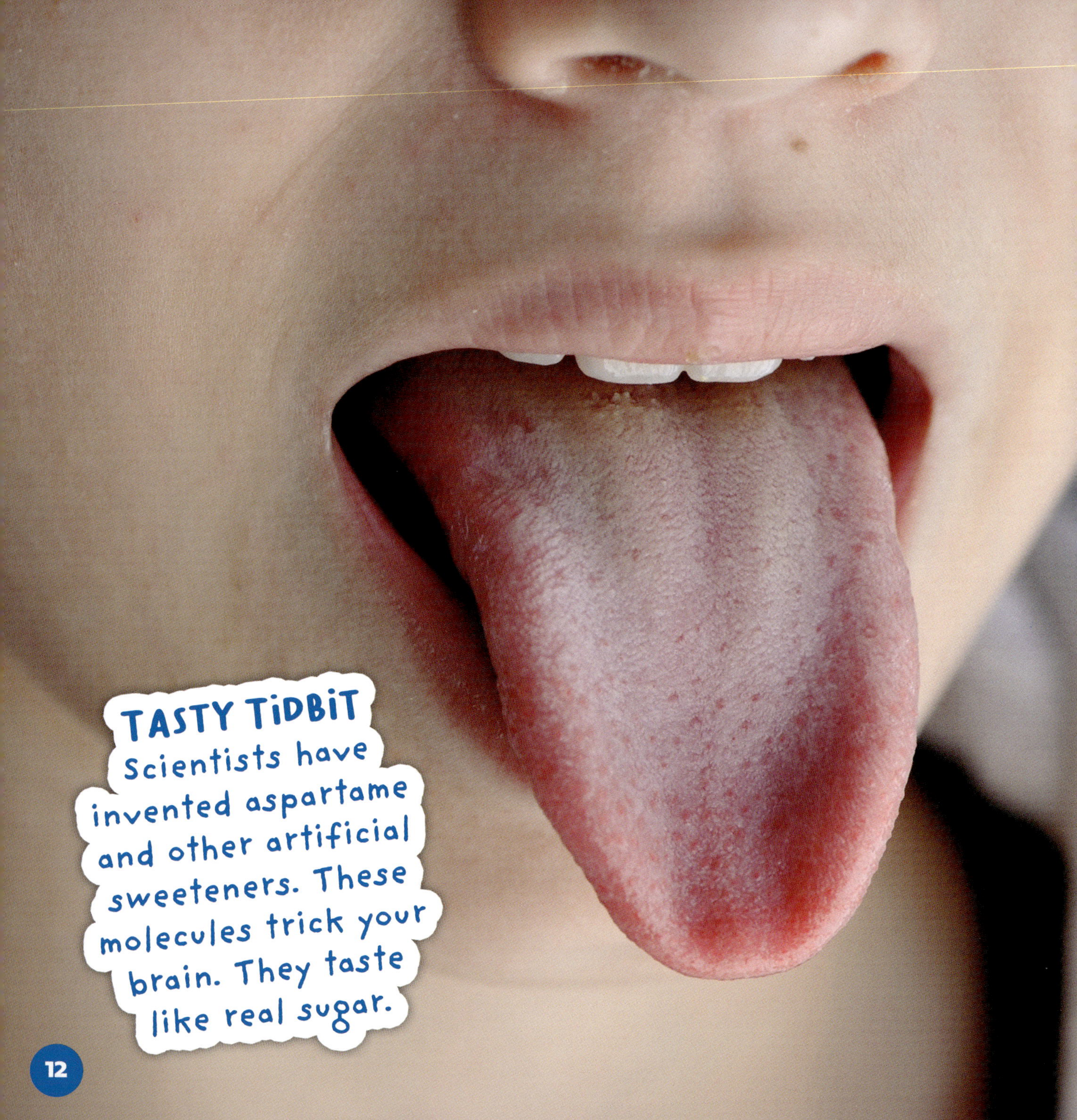

TASTY TIDBIT

Scientists have invented aspartame and other artificial sweeteners. These molecules trick your brain. They taste like real sugar.

Your tongue is covered with bumps called **papillae**. These are not taste buds. Taste buds are tiny structures inside papillae.

Each taste bud is shaped like a pocket. Tiny hairs called microvilli stick out. They sense sugar molecules. They send **signals** to the brain. That's how you know you are tasting something sweet!

Taste buds can detect five flavors. Sweetness is one. The others are sour, salty, savory, and bitter. It's not true that different areas of your tongue taste different flavors. All five flavors can be sensed all over your tongue.

TASTY TIDBIT
You have about 10,000 taste buds. Older people have less. That's why flavors taste stronger to kids than they do to adults.

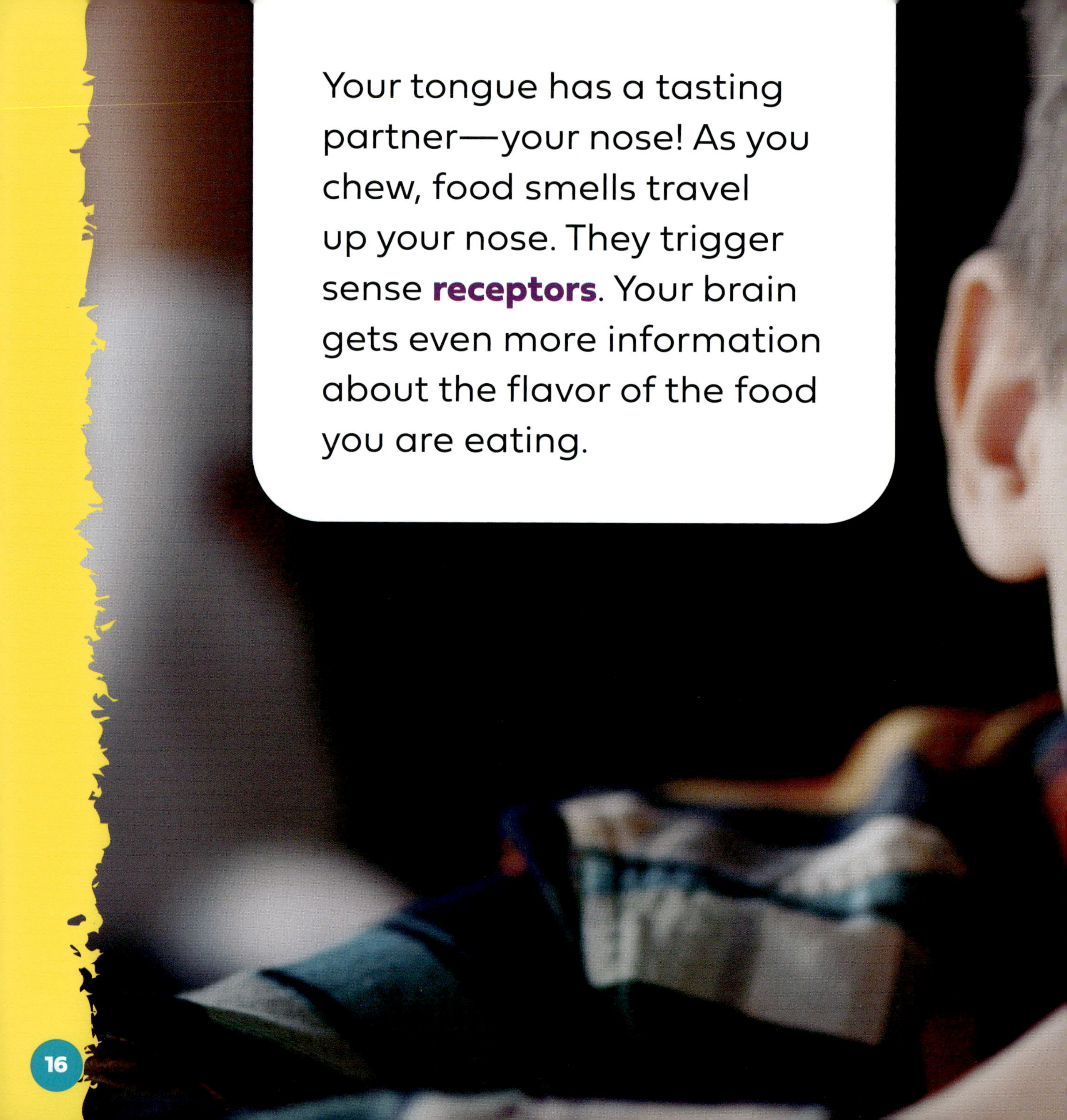

Your tongue has a tasting partner—your nose! As you chew, food smells travel up your nose. They trigger sense **receptors**. Your brain gets even more information about the flavor of the food you are eating.

TASTY TIDBIT
When you have a stuffy nose, you may have a hard time tasting your food.

Chapter Three

EATING SWEETS

Most people like sweet foods best. To understand why, it helps to think about human history.

Foods with a sweet flavor have lots of **calories**. They are rich in energy. Long ago, our ancestors had trouble finding enough food to survive. Sweet foods were rare. People lucky enough to find them had a big advantage.

Sweets are no longer rare, but people still **crave** them. Today, the challenge is to eat them in **moderation**.

Eating too much sugar is bad for you. It can make you overweight. It can lead to **diabetes**. Make sure that yummy sweets are only occasional treats.

ROCK CANDY

Ingredients:

One to three wooden skewers

6 cups plus one tablespoon granulated sugar

2 cups water

Food colors or flavoring extracts (optional)

Clean glass jar

One clothespin for each skewer

Plastic wrap

Directions:

1. Sprinkle one tablespoon sugar on a plate. Wet the top half of each skewer and roll it in the sugar. Let dry completely.
2. With an adult's help, bring the water to a boil in a saucepan on the stove. Add six cups of sugar, one cup at a time. Stir to dissolve each cup before adding more. When all the sugar is dissolved, remove from heat. If you like, stir in food coloring or flavoring extracts.
3. Let the sugar syrup cool completely. Pour into the jar.
4. Use a clothespin to suspend each skewer upside down in the jar. It should stay about one inch (three centimeters) from the bottom of the jar. Cover the jar with plastic wrap. Put it in a cool, dark place for about three hours.
5. Use a fork to crack the top layer of crystals and release each skewer. Let the candy dry for a few hours before eating. Yum!

GLOSSARY

calories (KAL-ur-eez) amounts of energy contained in food

crave (krave) to want something very much

diabetes (dye-uh-BEE-teez) a disease in which there is too much sugar in the blood

moderation (mah-duh-RAY-shuhn) in reasonable amounts that are not excessive or extreme

molecules (MAH-luh-kyoolz) the smallest units that a chemical compound can be divided into; groups of atoms

papillae (puh-PILL-ee) small bumps on the tongue that contain taste buds

processed (PRAH-sesd) made or changed in a factory; unnatural

receptors (ri-SEP-turz) nerve endings that are sensitive to stimuli in the environment such as smells

refined (ri-FINED) purified and processed in a factory

signals (SIG-nuhlz) chemical and electrical messages that get sent to the brain through the body's nervous system

FURTHER READING

Highlights. *The Ultimate Science Cookbook for Kids: A Cookbook for Young Scientists That Transforms the Kitchen into a Food Lab for Learning*. Highlights Press, 2025.

King Arthur Baking Company. *Sweet & Salty!: King Arthur Baking Company's Cookbook for Young Bakers.* Simon & Schuster Books for Young Readers, 2025.

ON THE INTERNET

Boston Children's Hospital: Facts about Sugar
childrenshospital.org/sites/default/files/media_migration/3e3d91bf-85b3-436d-b081-ac9f161b1b96.pdf
Learn about the effects of sugar on your body.

Children's Hospital of Pittsburgh: The Sugar Show
youtube.com/watch?v=WDgDWFEPdYg
Learn about sugar-sweetened drinks and how to make healthy choices.

INDEX